BIBLE VERSE

GREETING CARD BOOK

This book contains 18 different greeting cards and an envelope pattern. The cards are ready to color, fold and send.

- 3 Valentine's Day Cards
- 2 Easter Cards
- 2 Get Well Cards
- 1 Thank You Card
- 1 Mother's Day Card
- 1 Father's Day Card
- 1 Grandparent's Day Card
- 4 Birthday Cards
- 3 Christmas Cards

by David and Elaine Cole

ISBN 1-883426-05-7

A Publication of
Children's Outreach
New Whiteland, In 46184

HOW TO MAKE A CARD

Cut the card out along the heavy line. Let the children color it. Fold along the first fold line. Be sure the pictures are to the outside.

Fold the card along the second fold line.

The card is ready to sign and place into an envelope.

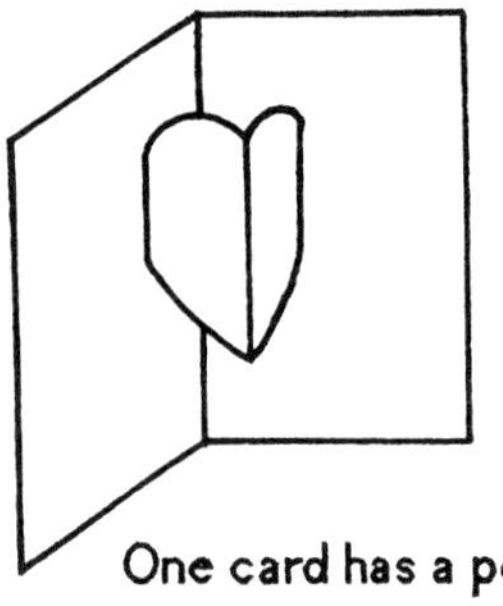

One card has a pop-up. Let the children color the card and make the first fold in it. Cut the heart out along the dashed lines. Lift the heart and make a fold from the point at the bottom to the center of the top. Carefully fold the card the final time.

HOW TO MAKE AN ENVELOPE

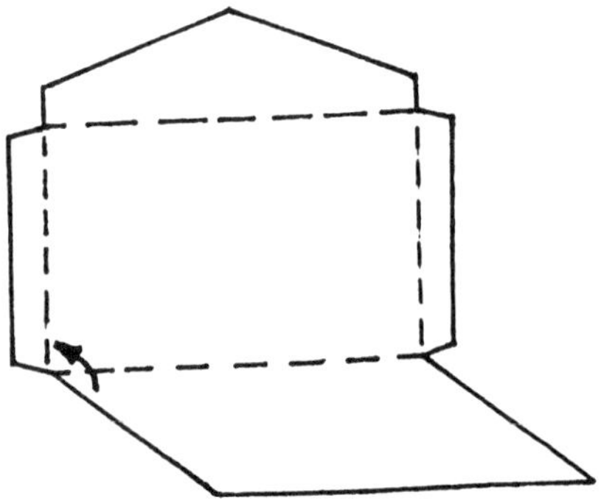

Trace or copy the envelope. Cut it out along the heavy line. Fold the bottom up at the dashed line. Make sure the dashed line is to the inside.

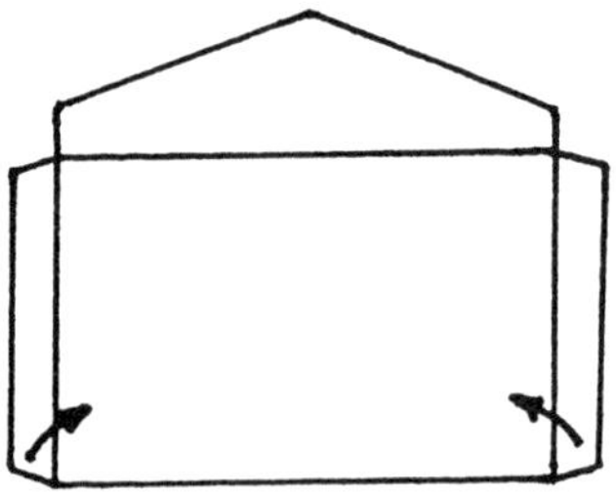

Put paste on the two side tabs. Fold them over onto the bottom tab.

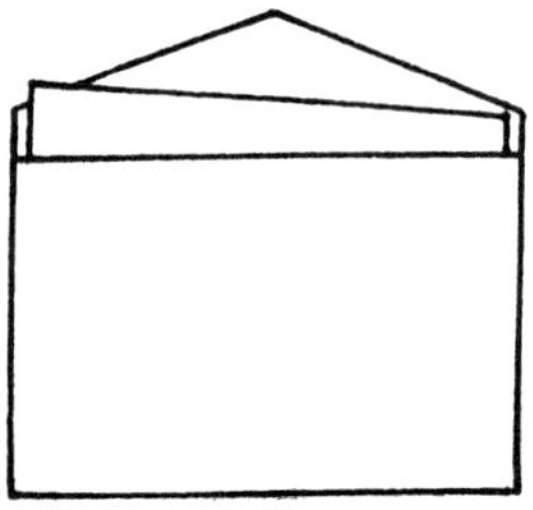

Place the card into the envelope. Fold the top tab over to close it.

Fold 2

God loves us
and gave His Son,
He died on the cross
for everyone

God is Love

Fold 1

Fold 1

Give Your Heart

to Jesus

Especially Made For You
Card

Happy Valentine's Day

Fold 2

Fold 2

Fold 1

Fold 1

Happy Valentine's Day

**Roses are red
violets are blue,
I love people
who are nice, like you.**

"A new com-
mandment I
give unto you,
That ye love
one another."
John
13 : 34
Jesus
loves
you

Please "Bee" My Valentine

Especially Made For You
Card

Fold 2

Fold 2

Happy Valentine's Day

On Valentine's Day
and all year through,
Jesus loves me,
and He loves you.

Fold 1

Fold 1

Hopping you'll be my Valentine

Especially Made For You Card

Fold 2

Fold 2

In the Bible
there is a story
and I know it is true,
Dear Jesus died
and rose again
for me and you

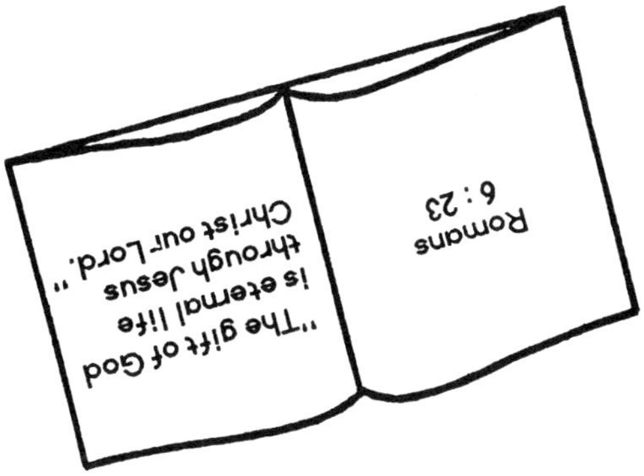

"The gift of God is eternal life through Jesus Christ our Lord."
Romans 6 : 23

Fold 1

Fold 1

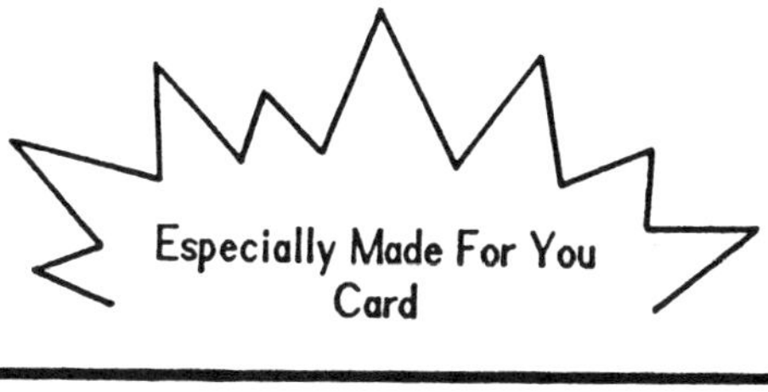

Happy Easter

Fold 2

Fold 2

On that first
Easter day,
Jesus rose to
take our sins away

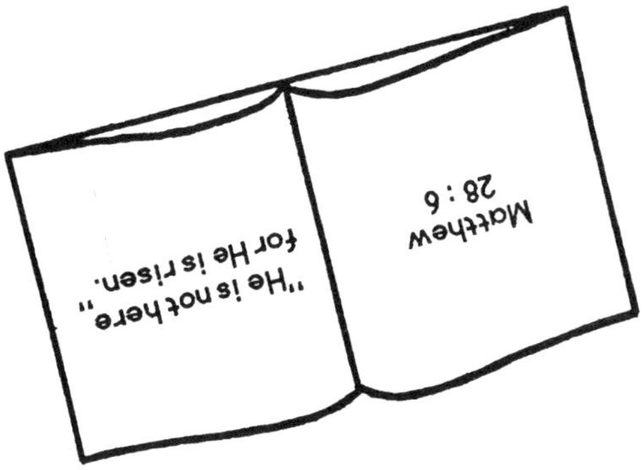

Fold 1

Fold 1

Happy Easter

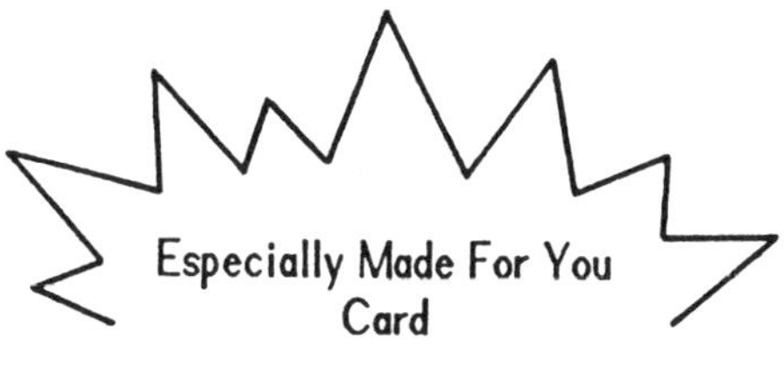

Fold 2

Fold 2

I pray being sick
will not last,
And you'll get
well real fast.

Get Well Soon

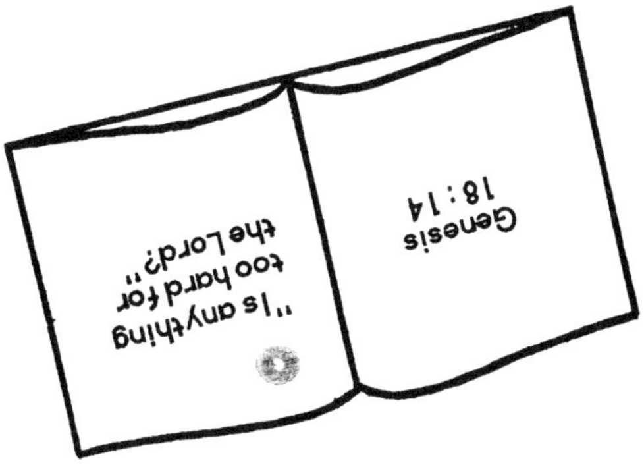
"Is anything too hard for the Lord?"
Genesis 18:14

Fold 1

Fold 1

I heard the Baa-
news
that
you
were
sick

Especially Made For You Card

Fold 2

Fold 2

Get Well Soon

"The Lord is my shepherd; I shall not want."
Psalms 23 : 1

I was sad to
hear you were sick,
I pray you'll
get well quick

Fold 1

Fold 1

Hopping
you'll
get
well
soon

Especially Made For You
Card

Fold 2

Fold 2

Thank You
"In every thing give thanks."
1 Thessalonians 5 : 18

Roses are red
violets are blue,
Thank you, for all
the nice things you do

Fold 1

Fold 1

Thank you very much

Especially Made For You Card

Fold 2

Fold 2

Happy Mother's Day

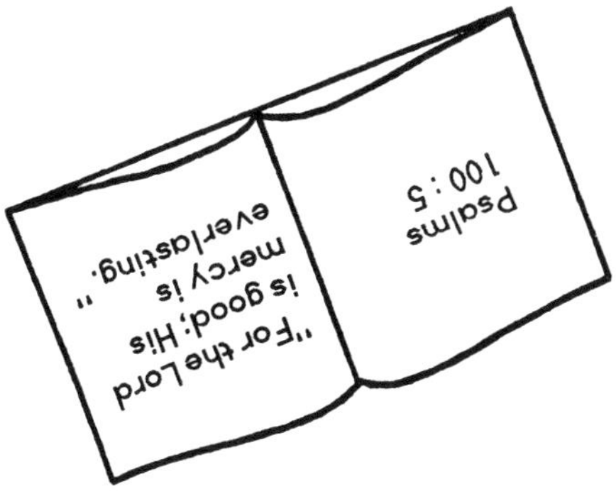

"For the Lord is good; His mercy is everlasting."
Psalms 100 : 5

I like flowers,
so nice to smell,
I love you, Mom,
and think you're swell.

Fold 1

Fold 1

Happy Mother's Day

Especially Made For You Card

Fold 2

Fold 2

Happy Father's Day

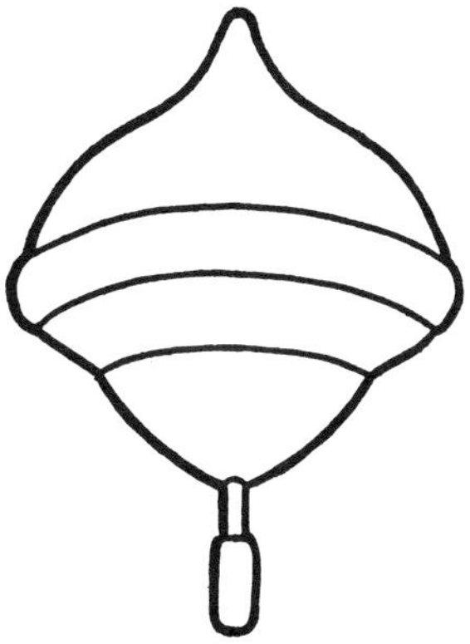

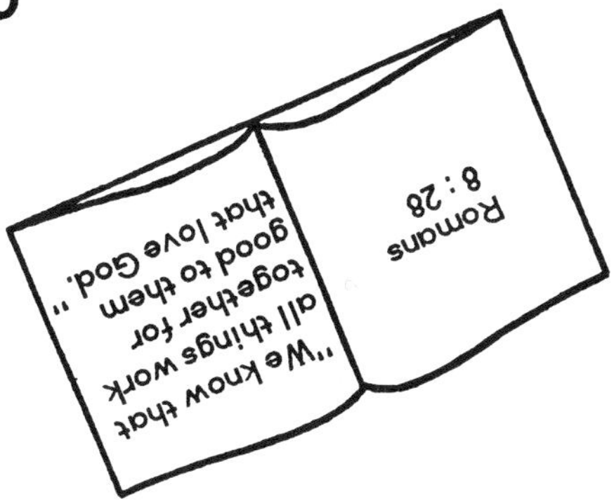
"We know that all things work together for good to them that love God."
Romans 8 : 28

When I think of someone I love, guess who's name is on the  You guessed right if you said my Pop.

Fold 1

Fold 1

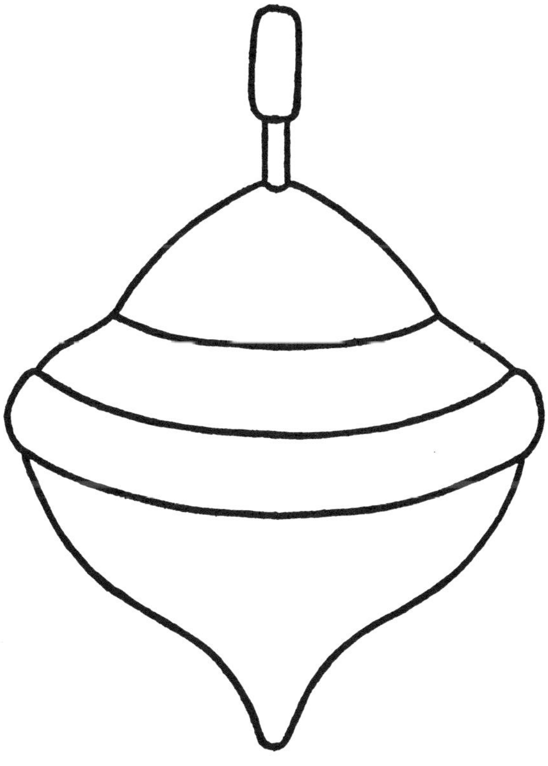

Especially Made For You Card

You're tops Dad

Fold 2

Fold 2

You're

grrr-eat

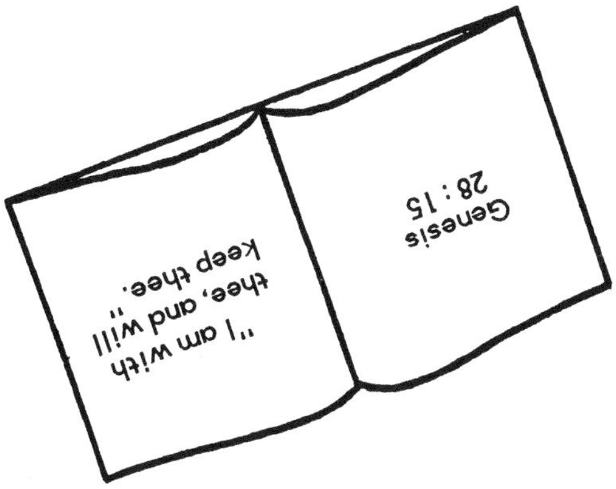
"I am with thee, and will keep thee."
Genesis 28 : 15

I love ice cream
and I love cake,
I love my grandparents
and think they are great.

Fold 1

Fold 1

I think

you're

grrr-eat

Happy Grandparents Day

Especially Made For You Card

Fold 2

Fold 2

Happy Birthday

I have a birthday
wish for you,
That it will be
purr-fect,
all day through.

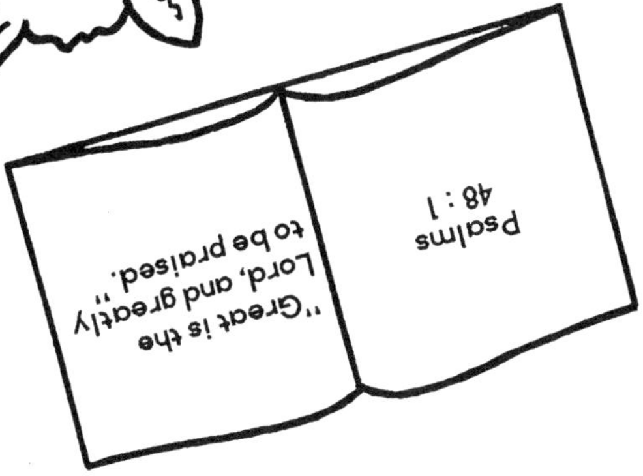
"Great is the
Lord, and greatly
to be praised."
Psalms
48 : 1

Fold 1

Fold 1

Have
a purr-
fect
birthday

Especially Made For You
Card

Fold 2

Fold 2

Happy Birthday

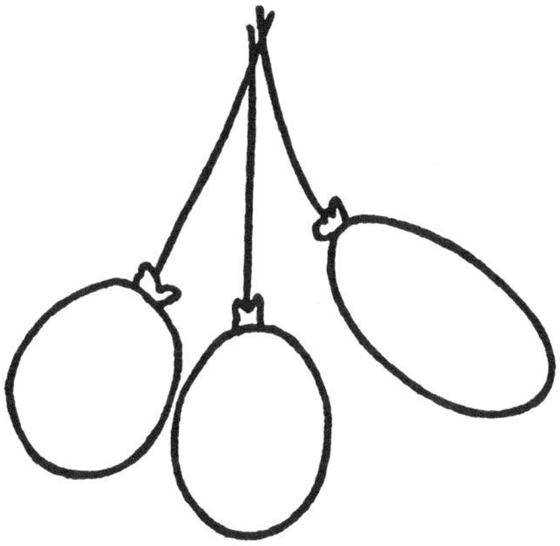

It's your birthday
and I'm so glad,
Hope you have the
best you've ever had

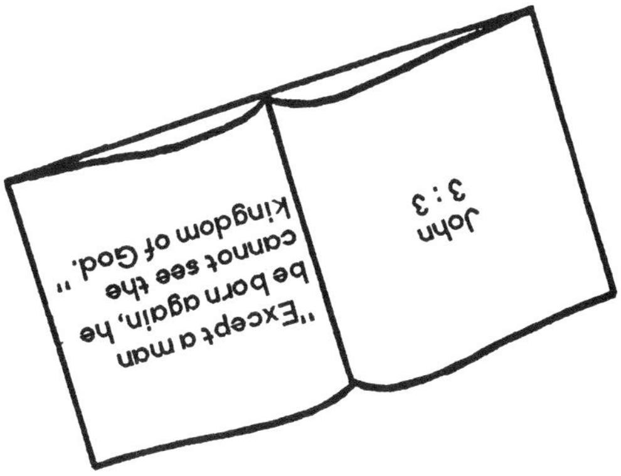
John
3 : 3
"Except a man
be born again, he
cannot see the
kingdom of God."

Fold 1

Fold 1

Happy
Birthday

Especially Made For You
Card

Fold 2

Fold 2

Happy Birthday

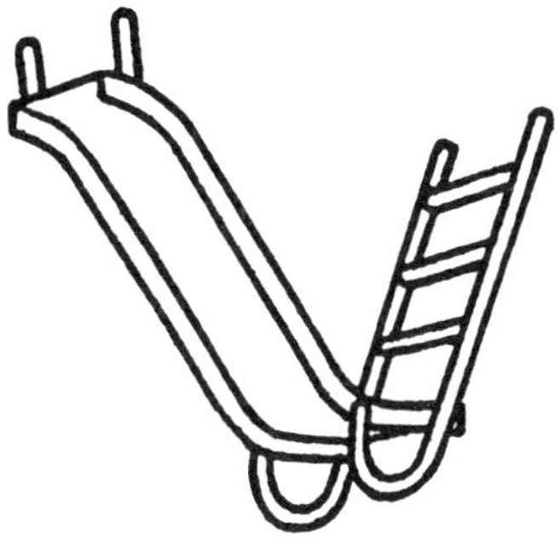

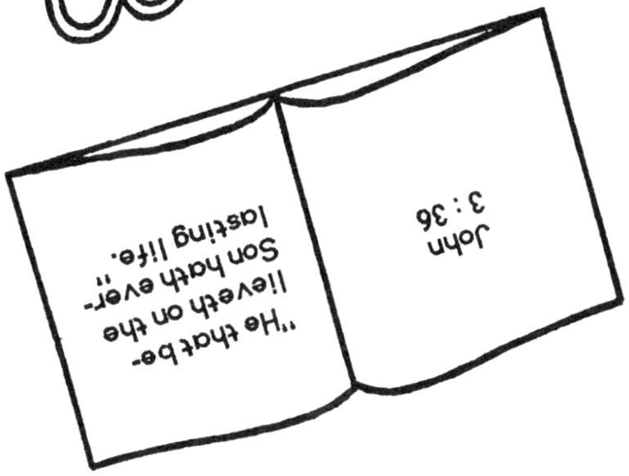

"He that be-
lieveth on the
Son hath ever-
lasting life."
John
3 : 36

This special day
must not slide by,
Without a big
birthday Hi!

Fold 1

Here's a line
to say
Happy Birthday

Especially Made For You
Card

Fold 2

Fold 2

This little card
sent your way,
is to wish you
a Beary
Happy Birthday

Happy
Birthday

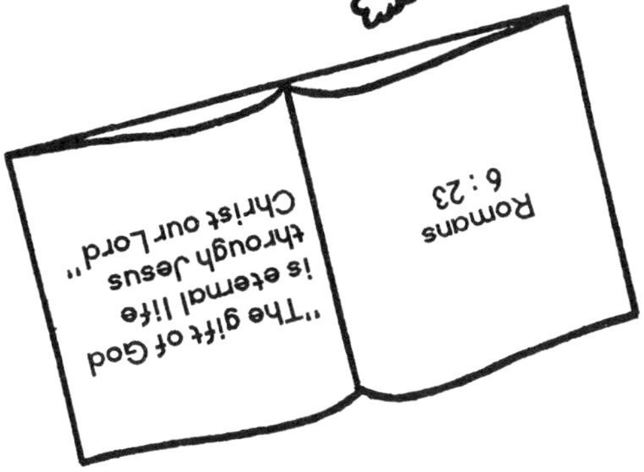
"The gift of God
is eternal life
through Jesus
Christ our Lord."
Romans
6 : 23

Fold 1 Fold 1

Have a
Beary
Nice
Birthday

Especially Made For You
Card

Fold 2

Fold 2

Especially Made For You Card

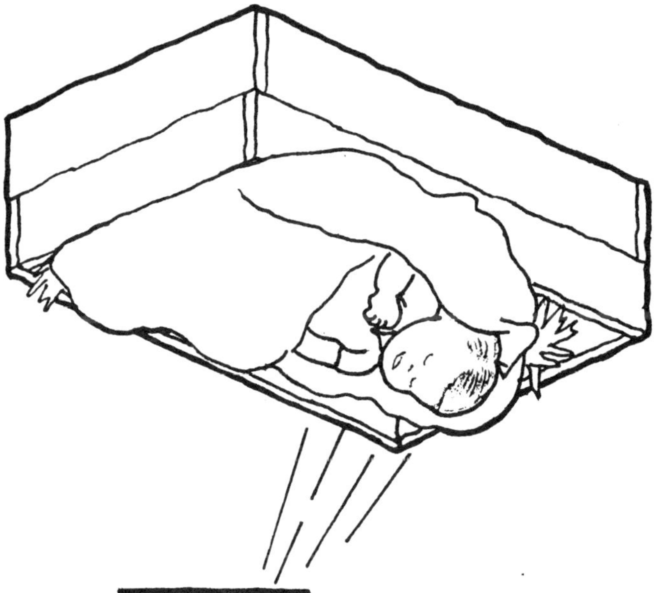

Have a Wonderful Christmas

Fold 1

Matthew 1 : 21
"Thou shalt call his name Jesus."

In a manger
baby Jesus lay,
God gave His gift of love
on Christmas day.

Merry Christmas

Fold 2

Fold 2

Merry Christmas

Christmas time is here
and I'm glad,
Merry Christmas
Mom and Dad.

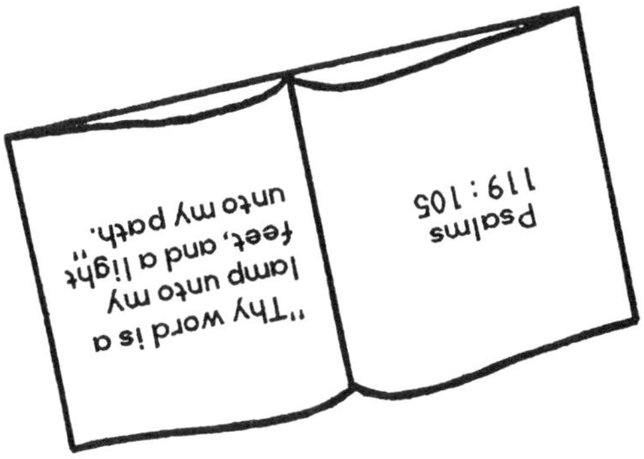

Fold 1 Fold 1

Have a very Merry Christmas

Especially Made For You Card

Fold 2

Fold 2

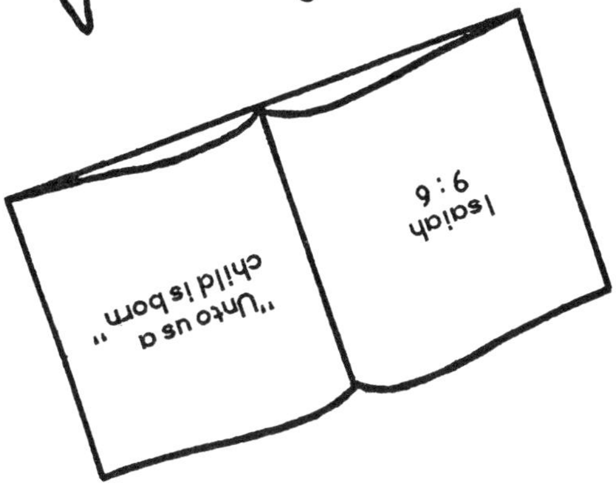

"Unto us a child is born"
Isaiah 9:6

In a land
across the sea,
Jesus was born
for you and me.

Fold 1

Fold 1

Merry Christmas

Especially Made For You Card

Fold 2

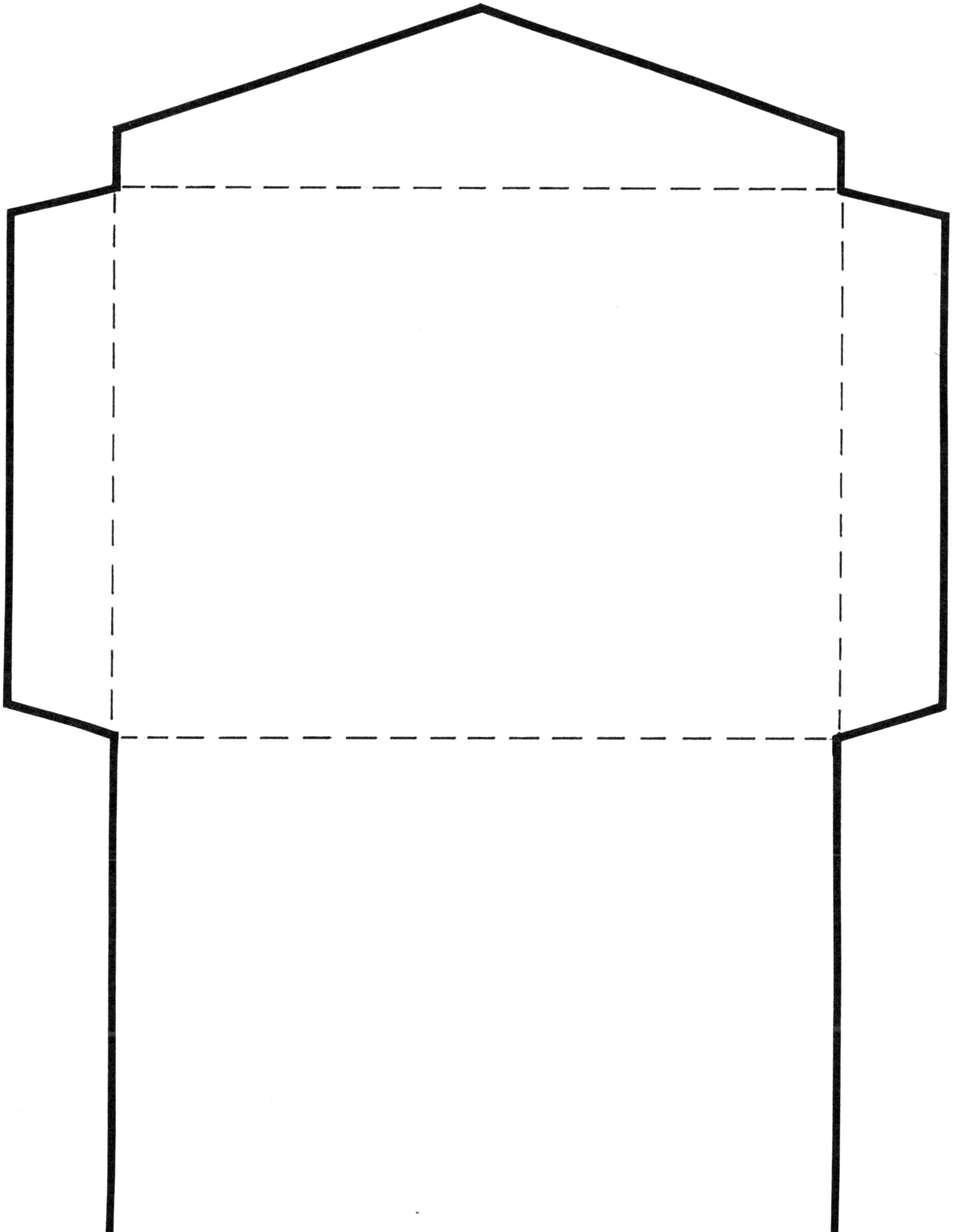